Museum of My Soul
The Time It Took

Written by:

Dornel Phillips
A.K.A
D-Nice Keoma

First Printing, 2020

ISBN: 978-1-7770824-0-6 (1st Edition Paperback)
ISBN: 978-1-7771543-0-1 (2nd Edition Hardcover)
ISBN: 978-1-7770824-9-9 (2nd Edition Paperback)

E-mail: dornel.phillips@gmail.com
www.dnicekeoma.com

Cover design by Dornel Phillips
Book design and production by Blurb.com
Editing by Michael Amobeda

Dedications

This book is dedicated to my parents, family, and friends. All those who have supported and encouraged me to keep writing. This book is dedicated to all those who've asked me to create a book of my poetry. This book was created with your inspiration and motivation in mind.

I also want to thank my university friends Gavin Holder and Michelle Palms. Gavin was the first person to encourage me to keep writing after sharing with him some of my first poems. Michelle encouraged me to do more with my poetry. She got me to do my first spoken word performance, which soon led to others. Thanks also go out to my former poetry collective Words by the Water. We were a great group of writers. During our time together I was able to work on my creativity as well as improve my ability as a spoken word artist. These individuals have all played a role in helping me develop as an artist.

This book is truly dedicated to every muse, encounter, and lover past and present. They've been some of the major inspirations for the relationship poems I've written over the years. I want to thank them all for the inspiration and the mirrors they presented to me. Each gave me a little bit of insight into what I needed to be better. Some ended good, and some not so well. This book is also dedicated to anyone whoever liked, shared my poetry or came to see me perform. Your support has been greatly appreciated over the years.

I hope this book in a small way captures some of the talent and potential my supporters have seen in me. And hopefully, I met those standards with this book. This is only the beginning, this is the first book of many more to come. I hope you'll come along with me on this journey

Thank you again to every supporter, for the love and encouragement. I hope you enjoy this small, but meaningfully collection of poems. I want you to enjoy this museum I call my soul

Table of Content

Table of Content

Section Titles	Page Number

Introduction

Museum of My Soul is a collection of poems that tells a love story. These poems cover the real dynamics of romantic relationships, seen through my eyes. The title Museum of My Soul, The Time It Took originates from the duration of time it took putting together a body of work that was both cohesive and told a story. The title also represents loosely a kind of relationship history. The museum of my soul in that sense is a collection of artifacts (poems) from different phases and periods of my life and relationships.

These poems were written over twelve years and show the difference is the thought process I had about relationships throughout that time. The dates in which each poem was written are not provided as this gives the collection a more cohesive feel of a story. Hopefully, the decision to so keeps you the reader engaged in the experience. As museums have different exhibits displaying different eras, regions, etc., so does the book. My goal is to highlight three sections in relationships, as per how I see it. The rise, climax, and fall, and this is shown through the three sections.

Many believe relationships to be a mirror, as do I. Our partners' acts a reflection of how we show up in the world. They show us the things we need to work on. Whether and how long those relationships last, is an issue for another conversation.

The three exhibits of this book are as follows

Exhibit A: Falling (The infatuation stages of early love)
Exhibit B: Being broken (Relationship acting as our mirrors, showing us our faults)
Exhibit C: Ending (When the relationship can no longer work and it comes to its conclusion)

I hope you enjoy your tour through the *Museum of My Soul*, enjoy your stay, and hopefully, you'll come again.

Museum of My Soul
is now

Enjoy your visit

The universe told me to open up
And show you the museum of my soul
So here I am open
For you to search, and behold
All the artifacts within me I hold
Each one filled with so much history
Giving small details of my internal mysteries
For which answers I'm still trying to find
Some facts might be fiction
That I've made up in my mind
But the reality may catch up
It's never too far behind

Museum of My Soul
The Time It Took:

Falling

SOCIAL MEDIA FEED

The thing I love about her is her smooth skin
As superficial as that may seem
Her body glows like
She lives in cream or lotion as some may call it
Her body reflects light, like sunlight shining on the ocean
And she's got the motion
The tone of a butter pecan tart
For her aesthetics alone, I'm lusting
Thinking I might be feeling something
In my heart that you and I might have an us thing
Misrepresenting this as a trust thing
Intentions like wet iron, kind of rusting
Superficial yeah, but I'm West Indian
No behavior
I draw inspiration to write from your social media feed
My appetite for beauty, you feed
Fantastical thoughts, you planted those seeds
But I stay flipping your pages you're such a good read
You give air, so I breathe
But back to the topic at hand
I'll keep daydreaming why I'm not your man
This is getting out, so damn
Why am I not?
Well I don't know you
So outside a double tap on your pictures
What am I to show you?

Be My Muse

Be my muse
My 5 o'clock evening news
You've had a long day
Let me you take off your shoes
Be my muse
You look hungry let me feed you food
Your soul needs nutriment
You already provide me with joy
And encouragement
Be my muse
Around you not one flower bend
I don't need a Barbie to my Ken
I need me a muse
Someone that can help me and I help them
We take each other to levels we've never been
Beyond queens, beyond kings
Only securing wins

Be my muse
My breaking news
That final play in the fourth
Seeing you, I really look forth
That guiding light you be my star in the north
Be my muse
Be my inspiration
Help me change a nation
Shining in bright situations
We'll never let it get dark
Be my muse

Be my heart
My life, I want you to remain being apart
Without you
This journey of success couldn't have started
So this connection, between us
Won't fall apart
Hold tight
It amazing having you hold me
Through the night
We argue and sometimes we fight
But we won't break
We're held together tight

Be my muse
Give to me life
Be my muse
Help me make this right
Just say yes
Be my muse
My breaking evening news
Be mine, muse
Everyone needs one
Even me, a silly fool

Black Magic

Black magic
No superstition, spells or potion
Just your black skin
Has got me feeling all these emotions
I want to fish in and out of your oceans

Black magic
With your mahogany nectar
Got me doing mathematic equations
Geometry, learning all your vectors
You're the place I want to inhabit
Study all your sectors

Black magic
Sprinkle some upon me
Black magic
Your skin is so lovely
Black magic
Because it's of you I'm thinking, love see
Whatever it is that you did
Keep doing to me
Black magic

Black magic
Your natural hairs
Your pearly whites
And your melanin, chocolate skin
Is what I want to be touching every night
I love, my lover's chocolate
So of you, I'm consuming every bite
Black magic
It just has to be, the way you just pop on my screen
Black magic
Now you just pop up when I dream
Black magic
You're perhaps the prettiest human being I've ever seen
Black magic
Your lips must be sugar, I need you to sweeten my tea
But I'll accept a kiss, if you agree
Black magic
Do your sorcery upon me
Black magic

You didn't need help
Falling for you has been automatic
Because you just being black is magic
And the spell of falling in love
It wasn't that at all
Just my habit
I love you black, magic

Ebony Flower

She's an ebony flower
That blooms by the hour
The attention of a room she consumes
That's her power
Building anticipation for her like towers
Sprinkling rain like showers

Like an ebony flower
A special kind of black
A mahogany rose, yes her type is that
Flower so exotic, birds of the aquatic
A once in a lifetime event
A special aroma it's not often you can smell
Such a beautiful scent

Ebony flower, never go sour
Always so sweet
The fragrance of the heavens and clouds
Ebony, on the strength of tropic trees
A flower that blows in tropic breeze
She the topic, her traits we're discussing these
She's everything
And her colour like her name is Ebony

An ebony flower
Something was missing in the world
Yes ebony there's a need for us
Florist, your thoughts
Your feelings let me be their tourist
Goddess Ebony exploring who you are
To me is very important
My ship in your dock I want to be porting

Like an ebony flower
Daydreaming of the hours
We spent in your flower bed
I want to pick and place you on my mantle
A flower so perfect, your nectar the bees
couldn't handle
Clean never involved in scandal
I see us on beaches, sunglasses, and sandals

Ebony rose
Only the heavens really know

How to get yourself one of those
Ebony dandelion
To catch your affection
One should never stop trying
I'm gonna get you,
This boy has never been one for lying
Ebony lily
Around you it's okay, I'm a little silly

Like an ebony flower
Your dark heavily melaninate complexion
Screams to me
That you must be the goddess of perfection
I feel between us an unspoken connection
You're the right one, I've made my selection
Ebony with a flower crown
Queen thanks for having me around
I'm so happy I found
My ebony flower

Moon Child

Like sunshine at the midnight hour
My dear moon child, you a Sun Flower
April reigns and May showers
I'm thinking pretentious thoughts
The hours go by with no answers
I need some of your gold powder
Cover me in your sparkling rays
My mind brings me back to you
A million times a day
I don't know what to think
You gave me a head nod and a wink
Somehow you got my emotions to grow
And not to shrink
We go through issues
But I'm still running the Nile
You can get what you want out of me
Just issue a smile
Pen to paper, I'm inking your style
I want to solve them, don't want our problems to pile
Because in resentment another issue is filed

Like sunshine at the midnight hour
You want things that are bright in the darkest hours
But sometimes there are no golden rays
Just white moonlight, giving limited visibility
Sometimes we've got to navigate the darkness
Without the aid of light
And have to trust in all that we've done
A belief that everything is going to be alright
My beautiful moon child
You a Sun Flower
I feel your strength
I can see your power
Love tips the scales by the hour
I only hope this construct we built
Don't break and turn sour

Just One Kiss

Just one kiss
Will have you reminiscing
About what you've been missing
About the power of what a kiss can do
When I place my lips upon you
The emotions that'll come through
I know you can't undo

A kiss
A single one
Will have your mind going through thoughts
Thoughts you forgot about me and you
The power of a kiss
The sweetness of another's lips
Can transport you
Take your mind and body on a trip
Without ever leaving this place

The lips that's all it takes
A kiss will break all constrains
As our lips and bodies embrace
We're addicted to the taste
Fascinated by that thing mounted on our faces
Located beneath our noses
And when yours touches mines
That's when I feel the closest, to you

Now I hope you now understand
What one kiss can do
And I can't wait
Well I'm hoping I can put my lips upon yours
And you'll see the power a kiss can have on you
The emotions that springs on you
I promise you can't undo
So let me put this kiss
My lips on you

Eyes

She told me it was my eyes
That got her so addicted
Trapped
Borderline restrictive
Addictive
Can't pay rent, evicted
To the passion of my mystery
She became a victim
Infatuation started in her head
Then started to spread all through her system

I was in her bloodstream
I invaded her body
A disease
But my symptoms were
Keeping alive my victims
Heartbeat racing
White blood cells unable to defend
The sensations she's chasing

Said it was my eyes that pierced her inhibitions
To come to me, a sign of intuition
Make her break the rules
Abandon all traditions
I told her I was not to be worshiped
But she made me into a religion
Flashes of life, a constant image in her visions

Said it was my eyes, the mystery
Said it felt like
We've known each other for a while
It was like we shared some form of
Forgotten history
Told her I was not the one
Said I didn't understand faith
This journey between us may have just begun
And this was just the introduction
We were still on
Said it was my eyes
That cut through all the bullshit and the lies
She Said I may honour you

But understand we don't have idle eyes
Nobody should be idolized
But that doesn't mean I shouldn't hold you
In high regard
That doesn't mean I shouldn't see you
As the god that you are
I said I'm honoured, but you're the god
You're a queen
Highest amongst us, human beings
With a smile she said
It's your eyes

Told me, it was my eyes
Told me that's where all our realness lies
The soul, the passion
Said she's a reserved woman
But my eyes made her take this action

My eyes
These were her words
Said my eyes told her
I could bring to her life satisfaction

Your eyes, she said
My eyes
It may have only been our first time meeting
But my eyes, she said
Got her addicted
Said she found the lover
Her whole life she has been seeking
All hidden within these eyes

His-Story of Her in The Making

This is history in the making
I want to capture you in a frame
No, you, I want to be painting
Like true artist do
I want to use my brush to interpret you
I want to use many colours
To highlight emotions
And express feelings
I want to take time with you
Making sure I got every detail right
I want to rework you for several nights
Until I think you're done
A completed work of art that's just right
I, then want to hang you on walls of galleries
Showing off your beauty for all eyes to see
Then I want to put you up for auction
Then outbid everyone
I'm going be your highest bidder
Then I'm going to take you home
And hang you on my bedroom wall
So I can see you each moment when I awake
This is love, not a fairytale that's been made up

Snap, snap
For who is this of whom I speak
For she's
She is special, she is habit
What she produces I've got to have it
She is everything, she is all things
She's art
She is music
She is beauty
She is joy
She is perfection
She's life
Certain things has rings to it
So she is wife

This is history in the making
I was asleep
But since finding you I've been awaken

Heavily invested in feelings has got me shaken
Paradise
From my words look what you have taken
This is a special kind of infatuation
This isn't an obsessive kind of situation
Just royalty finding royalty
Soul connections, respect, and affection
Loyalty all for you, all in me
His story in her making
Love between two gods
God and goddess
King and queen
That's what we're building
Something that was once only a dream

Light Brown

You're the perfect shade of light brown
Others were wrong, but you right now
Right down, to the shoes on your feet
Not to mention your fragrances that be so sweet
You're like that summertime breeze

You're a perfect shade of light brown
I never knew I needed you
But I'm needing you right now
You're life, for me
The raft that keeps me afloat
In the stream of life's rough currents
I want you as my one and only, my last
More than just my current
Is that not apparent?
Excuse my incoherence
Through my hearts border control
I'm granting you all clearance

You're the perfect shade of "like" brown
A special force, pound for pound
Never knew what I wanted, but I have it now
You're more than a phase, you're a habit
How?
How did you get to me?
My heart and my soul, now wanting you excessively
What did you do?
Why didn't others have this recipe?
I wish I knew
Still trying to learn what this lesson be
No matter the methods, we stay connected
Some of the things you do has got me all types of effected

You're the perfect shade of light brown
You're my queen, you wear the crown now
I guess there's no going back
I'm in love, wow!

Tell Me

Tell me what I've been missing
I'm here baby just to you listen
Can't take my eyes off those lips I've been kissing
Need you close, don't want the distance
I was the same, hope for you I can be different
You gave me game, and I'll do the same
Making love breaks the pain
No tattoos on our bodies
But my thoughts are written all over your brain

Tell me baby and I'm gonna listen
That's how we grow
Communication is important, so
Lemme hear what's on your mind
You got my ears and my time
Your soul, I wanna mine
I'm digging you
Trying to go deeper
There's nothing sweeter
Than to watch you sleep near my heart
I'm willing to accept that you might break it in parts
Lying with you naked in the dark
Thinking every story has an arc
And this ours

I'm willing to risk the heartbreak
An outcome I will not run from
To love, one must be vulnerable on all fronts
It's your game, I'm merely playing my part
Just tell me where and I'll start
Tell me, baby, share what's in your heart

Fallen

I'm falling faster and harder for you
Than a stone dropped in the middle of the ocean
Meaning these emotions have got me sinking
And lately
It's been only of you I've been thinking
These feelings are so revealing
My hearts' bruised ain't no way of healing

Yet still, I fall deep and fast in love with you
Like a rock thrown into a lake
In love with me, I hope you I'd make
I don't care how long this takes
Making you my woman
I have too long waited
Why am I feeling this way?
Well you made me
Made me see you in a new light
Made me feel that with you
Things would be just right
Made me understand
Whatever happened that was just life
And there was no need to be down, cause strife
With you, everything was so nice

Falling like a skydiver from a plane
Meaning the way I feel about you is almost insane
Being with someone else will not be the same
There's no depth for you I won't reach
There's no distance for you I wouldn't travel
Because I've fallen so hard, I can't get up
I'm rattled
To love someone is an internal battle

I'm falling
But it seems like I've already fallen
Flat on my face, a victim of this heart chase
My heart rate beats at a fast pace
Cause it's from logic that my mind and heart race
Falling, I've fallen victim to your charm
Your smile, your stare, your perfect hair
Your beauty, beautiful to me you are truly
And I'm newly, in love

But you're the one, I've waited all my life for
You are cupids' gift to me
Cause the way I feel about you
Gives to me joy I never knew
That's why I've fallen so fast, so hard for you
I've fallen complete overboard
That's why of you, I'm so sure
I'm in love

Premonition

I had a vision in my head
Of you laying in my bed
So seductive
Uninterrupted
The thought so disrupting
Now you know right away
How this brighten up my day
You're special is what I'm trying to say
Then a ray of light from the sun
Hits my face and my dream was done
But I couldn't help myself from harping back
On how your love puts me on
And then at the same time, takes me off track
Yes, just like that

I had a vision
Of you naked in the kitchen
You were on the counter
Producing heat like the stove
High heels on exposing your pedicure toes
Yes this vision was one of those
X rated

I had a vision, a premonition
Yes thoughts of you
Are what got me in this condition
Thinking of you in positions
Call the physician
Because the way you're bending in my head
Is giving me glee
From this dream, I don't want to freed
And I'm such feral lad
Yes a wild boy, mad
I had visions in my head
Your skin, reflecting sunlight
You're perfection done right
Come give me life
But I'm just dreaming
Waking, knowing it's only a matter of moments
Before you're back in my arms
Blessing me with your charms

You know I love you
Because just the simple thought of you
Is causes me to rise

A Love Philosophy

You dropped a pebble into the oceans of my soul
Causing endless ripples
Got me affected more than just a little
Water came up and splash right back down in the middle
After that why would anyone settle?
The effect of you has got me affected
It was destiny how we connected
Destiny why are you so eclectic?
Déjà vu, I think I love you
I don't know what is that you do
Must be your spell, your special kind of voodoo
That you do, so well
I've fallen into your waters stuck in your well
The ripples you caused are still moving, oh well
What you've done to me, don't tell
What you've done for me, there's no telling
We fell in love with a slow jam in a hotel inn
The feeling went for so-so to something so real

I'm not a religious man in any shape or form
But that's doesn't shape my norms when it comes to you
Do you not hear the praises I give to you?
On my knees, I pray it's to you
This is just a fraction of the things I'm willing to do
Not for me, just for you
So let me indulge in your sins
Even failure, with you, is still a win
Be my queen, let me earn the position of your king
Willing to give you every ring
For that pebble, you dropped in the oceans of my soul
Well it still rippling
And the emotions caused, crippling
Now I can't let you go
Now I've got to let you know
That's a love philosophy
Not Plato, but Van Gogh

Gospel To My Soul

You're the gospel to my soul
You fill me up with your magic
I'm now covered, with goals
I never know what to make of the stories
Of you I've been told
You were created by a master of craft
But you broke the mold
Rode your wave without a boat
It's no surprise you float
With no fear of sinking
You helped reshape my thoughts
My way of thinking
You're my linchpin
Yeah a major key thing
I've got you, you've got me
I need no further convincing

Your shadow is a light
You shine in dark places without the aid of sight
You're strong, your love is might
Got me flying beyond the fear of heights
Searching for electrics
Like kites being flown in thunderstorms at night
No wrongs, just right
No writers' block for you, I just type
The one for me, my type
Some are alive, but not living
These sensations, thank you for giving

Brought forth from you is a fire that entices
It's because of you I understand now
What my purpose in this life is
What is the just price, for such a priceless commodity?
In the theatre of my mind, you provide the comedy
Sometimes to pain that's the perfect remedy
Let's end this, no more harping on your sweet melodies
For the songs you sing from within your soul
Is giving me all this energy

Divine

You are so divine
Let me undress your mind
Let me see the nakedness of your thought
Deep conversation with each other let's set off
In mental stimulation let's get lost
Let's fool around with the imagination
Let your mind give birth to new creations

You're so divine
Your intellect is what makes you so refined
I want to discover the things you carry upon your mind
Only topics about you I want to find
Want to rhyme
Because it's you I'm interested in all the time
Let's undress your insecurities
And dress you up in some new confidence
Relax, don't be tense
Enjoy your life, make new friends

You're so divine
You've got a gold mind
The goal make you mine
I love sharing with you, you're time
I now know why it is you shine
Don't fall for these corny lines
But
You're so beautiful
Your thoughts make the body full
Intrigued by what you're thinking makes my body pull
Closer, together with yours
With you
I'll never, leave a conversation undone
Because what we've got here is just beginning
Nowhere close to thinking of an ending

Essence

I love your essence
Your style and your reverence
Your scent and your presence
Your smile is always so pleasant
You're that lucky number 7
That full house in poker
A superstar, no jokers
The closer
I need to you, be closer
You're paradise within a human frame
All the things you are can't be named
Stronger, than hurricanes
Stronger, pleasant like summer rain
Stronger, it's because of you that I became

A star without the fame
A star, your bright light can't be changed
Never go out, never go dull
My poetry, words
Transcends these pages
To form a painting upon a canvas
That is reflected in you in reality
Capture that, your spirituality
Find it in yourself, royalty
Your majesty
Imagine me, by your side
Its magic I see, within the twinkles in your eyes
You're my truth, others be the lie

I love your essence
Your style, that's your presence
Never gets old, your relevance
One of a kind, you got that special type of shine
Goals in you, I hope to find
Treasures, your heart
The price of diamonds
Bound by hope
Bathing in love
You can keep me clean, you're the soap
My lifeline, you're the rope
I'm the Vatican and you the pope
When I'm down you help me cope

Your essence
Your essence
From you, I've learned lessons
I cannot forget your scent
You loved me even when I didn't have a cent
A constant presence in my life
Your essence isn't just something I like
I love having you in my life
The essence that makes every wrong, right

Skin

Your skin upon my skin, I really like that
Kissed me upon my lips
Told me you'd be right back
Time with you is my favorite part of the day
You're my nightcap
You're an inspiration
You caused me to write that
When my life is feeling down and dark
You're the light that
Shines upon the beauty of my life
A sight to be seen
Yes, you give me that
A gift from above, a gift filled with love
Baby, you are that

A treasure, those are the facts
A museum of knowledge, a golden artifact
You are art, in fact, your beauty
Yeah there's art in that
I found you while digging for my soul
And found you, shimmering gold
And I had to keep you all for myself
You just couldn't be sold
You were the beauty of legends
The stories I've been told

Your head upon my shoulder
With your hand upon my chest
You make me feel strong
When you lay upon me to rest
Reasons why I love you
Well it's simply because you're the best
If I looked in a dictionary
A picture of you
Would be beside the word happiness
What have we missed?

Your skin upon my skin
I really like that
You're the type that
Makes someone like me feel happy

From the moment I laid eyes upon you
You knew that you had me
You're good for me
Baby you got the right wrap
Love it was hard to believe
But I just can't fight that
And when you kiss me goodbye
I always know you'll be right back
You holding me, I really like that
Your skin is upon my skin
And we're wrapped in the pleasures
Of the minds, bodies, and souls we're in
And that's closest to perfect
My life has ever been
Touching upon your skin

Nectar

Sweet nectar, blessed upon skin
A truly radiant glow
You're more than a star
You're its core, outwardly pouring
A life giver that requires more than just exploring
All are welcome local and foreign
Your gravity got me around your orbit
Death at depths there no need to be morbid

Heavenly, rains of light
Shining so bright
Making night time into day
A meteor of emotions
A shooting star of life
Your astrology says everything is just right
And like a new star, I want to be in your nebula
Brief moments, only for a brief moment

Sweet nectar, poured up skin
Sweet nectar, spread it on thick don't want it too thin
Sweet nectar, more than just skin
Sweet nectar of the fruit you claim as you
Sweet nectar, I want to taste that which you are covered in
I wouldn't mind having the experience of enjoying that
Sweet nectar, sweet nectar from this planetary soil

Galactic flames
Light speeds of thoughts
I hope the dark energy doesn't pull us apart
For you're my light in a space that is dark
Hope is what for you I've capture within my heart
It's a journey but I was ready
To ride the rocket from the start
Blasting off
And this just leads back to the soil
Back to the grounds where this all started
Back to the earth
Where in my mind you reign supreme
You're an amazing human being
And I can enjoy your nectar once more

Unruly

I love it when your hair is unruly
I love it that way truly
I love seeing you without makeup
When you wake up
Or if we're just chillin'
I love being around you
You give me a special kind of feeling
You know I said this time and time before
But I love that got damn fro of yours
You look the sweetest when it ain't the neatest
Maybe it's because I'm used to seeing an amazing individual
Like yourself always dressed up
That I don't often get to see the real you
The person underneath
Top to bottom no matter what, you're always sweet
See when you're dressed down, and your hair is unruly
No makeup on, it does something to me
It sends a sensation right through me
That's when you're not trying to impress anybody
That's when I knew you were comfortable
Being yourself around me
You've always been comfortable in your own skin
Discomfort with who you are has never been a thing
But when you're able to let your guards down around me
Well I find that to be a beautiful thing
You're beautiful, even in sweat pants and hair unruly
I love you for you, truly

Unruly Too

I love it when your hair's unruly
I love it that way truly
I love it in the morning when you wake up with no makeup
I love the minutes and the hours of my day that you take-up
I hate it when we break up
But love the moments after we spend when we makeup

I love your hair unruly
It just does something to me
It says you're comfortable being around me
It says you can be you and you're down see
With you, anything we do, we discuss it as a unit first
On any list, you, I'm putting on it first
I know I found my one, I don't have to search

I love it that at times you can be unruly
Your attitude does something to me
We fight sometimes, you're right most times
But that's life and to me, you're so kind
Just by breathing, you shine
I've fallen for you, not once but more than two billion times

Bedtime

At nights when I lay in bed and not asleep
It's you that I think of, not of sheep
The thought of you brings me comfort when my mind is strong
But my heart is weak

At nights when sleep escapes me
It's because the love I have for you awakes me
And it takes me, mentally to places I don't often go
And these emotions are something that I don't often show
But I love you, kinda
I'm guessing that something you ought to know
That's just something that I wanted to show
It's not a feeling that goes away it's something that often grows
I want to be with you because everywhere with you my heart will go

At nights when I lay my head down to sleep
I take comfort in you my sweet
You're all I see when I close my eyes to sleep
It just works that way, that you're the one for me
I like this feeling, this feeling that you give to me
Being in love with you is good, is good for me
You're that dream that I always dream of when I sleep
You're my dream but somehow whenever I awake
The sight of you is always twice as sweet
My love for you is something to keep
Yeah that's right my love for you
It's kind of deep
That's why I dream of you every night at bedtime
When it's time to sleep
Hoping that through the night your love for me you'll always keep
That's all I ask every night before I lay my head down to sleep
That you'll always be there, be there for me

Museum of My Soul
The Time It Took:

Being Broken

Artificial Feelings

Artificial feelings
No ways of doing real healing
Misunderstandings the ways we see things
You love with your mind, I love with the chest
You built up walls
My pride wants to knock them down
Passionate, but don't want to seem insecure
When I say I'm needing more

We can't see what the other needs
Only caught in our thoughts about how we feel
How did a romance that started above the clouds
Fall so far we're struggling to achieve any form of healing
Remembering it's humans with whom we're dealing
In a fast-paced world, artificial emotions are what we're sharing

We don't know how to work things out
We don't know the right ways, so we conceal things
If it ain't right in the moment
It has no worth, the given reason
Feelings
I guess it'll never be
I guess we're all children of broken emoting
See
Relationships
Page one, emergencies

Museum of My Soul

The Feeling

The feeling is just
You're not telling me much
It's killing me to touch
Fiendish for something I've never had
Don't know why I want you so bad
The feeling is lust
Can't conceive what is trust
Already painted me a picture with a dirty brush

Never wanted to desire
The queen of the fire
Watery flames stain the walls with your name
Stuck in the rot of rust, never wanted to change
Fame of intimacy, mimicking isolation
I see joy, but it's all frustration
We stood on no solid ground, failed to build a foundation
Placed ourselves in a futile situation
Nothing about us is regal, barely on side of the law, legal
Transparent but nothing we ever see through
Twisted, the things we do to get straight to the point
But we've lost ourselves, we've got no points

And that just a feeling

Make-Believe

I live in the land of make-believe
Maybe that's why I gotta make-belief
That you love me
Always wanting the best for me
Thinking of me
Things I tell myself
To not face the objective reality
That, that might not be how you feel
So I gotta make-believe, you love me
Really, really for real
Delusions, don't wanna accept this is how rejection feels
Peeling the layers of these emotions like an onion
Once pulled back this cannot be undone, no second opinions
Maybe it'll work out in the long run
But it took a long time, just to get here
My life has been a blur, wish with me you still shared
Yet still, I tell myself
To you, the way you feel about me is still unclear
You're just trying to sort out your fears

I make believe it
That you love me
But just don't say it
I'm living in a lie
Devilish cries
Your fixes to me do not apply
Cause I don't wanna be honest with myself
When my make-believe world feels so much better
Hope you can read my tears, with my love in every letter

Protect Your Heart

My, my, she had the prettiest brown eyes
Round thigh, umpire
Had to strike me out
I couldn't leave her side
She wore joy around her neck
And tattooed beautiful across her soul
Traveled the world
But far from cold
I found warmth in her
When everywhere else had been closed

Protect your heart, I've been told
But with her, I took the risk
I wanted to be bold
For she was the test that I wasn't afraid of failing
Cause even in the attempt
There was the benefit of potentially finding perfection
In our connection
The only regret I would have is not trying
I fell into the ocean of bliss within her eyes
She's captured my heart
Even if I failed to capture the prize of her love
She's away from me
But she's all I can think of
Even if this is just a brief moment in time
I'll cherish it for all eternity
True love is so hard to find
However, in my mind, she'll always be my mine

So how does one protect their heart
My mind has also fallen under her spell
I've fallen, I fell
Knowing this might not end well

One-sided Love affair

It's probably because I cared
When I shouldn't have
It was just an affliction of the mind
Wanting something that I couldn't have
But this feeling that I have just wouldn't pass
It keeps a hold on me
And I kept believing a feeling like this wouldn't last
Deep are my fantasies in the trenches of my mind
And they get deeper with time

It was probably because I cared
I know I never should have taken it there
But it probably was the glare that came off of you
And made me stare
I wanted something that I couldn't have
In reach but I couldn't grab
Wanted a hold of it
Just couldn't find the source of it
But the source of it was me
Created it in my thoughts
Now it's stuck in there like it's been super glued
The thoughts from which I can't escape is, of you

I can't have you
So I dream
Fantasies masquerade on my brain
As my subconscious always leads back to emotions lying dormant
That all I really seem to want is you

But these are dreams that won't come through
I'm lost haven't got a clue of what I'm gon' do
But this is just how the power of the brain plays tricks on you
That's just the effect
Falling for something can have on you
That's just what a one-sided love affair will do
When you love someone, who doesn't even notice you

Everything That I Lack

I kissed your lips hoping I could get a taste of your medicine
Now your antidote floats in my throat
Drowning, trying to swim up to your boat
But you won't give me an inch of rope
So I don't know if I can hope
To be saved by my misrepresented ideas of love
I can't find a way to your shores
Treading in misery, trying to keep my head above
This thing called foolish love
For they say only the foolish love
And fallen, a fool in love
For it's you I love
But stain emotions, like grape juice on white t-shirts
These two things don't fit right
With you, it's like
We fight to remain intact,
You're everything that I lack
But there's very little click, click
So it's hard to know if we're capturing the picture right
I venture to the moon just to sit on your satellites
Ventured to the sky so the stars won't have to sleep alone at night
Upon Saturn, I once peered with spite
For its seven rings
And I just wanted to gift you one

Now I see the light
Blinded, now I feel the fright
Take me to the highest heights
Beyond the clouds, beyond the stars
Beyond the darkest spaces, beyond lights
Show me the god in you,
Show me what your piece of god is like
Show me what I've done wrong
Because for you I want to be what's right

She Loves me, She loves me not

She loves me
She loves me not
She loves me
She loved me lots
She loves me
Then she loves me not
She loves me
Then she loves me in spots
She loves me
Then her love for me tends to stop

See this woman has got me picking
At the pedals of flowers for hours
Trying to figure out
Exactly about me how she feels
She knocks me back, I'm on my heels
Got me thinking she's loveless, nerves of steel
I think she loves me
Then I think she loves me not
Arrested my emotions
For dealing my feelings on the block
On my heart, I think she's called the cops
Digging graves in my mind
Every day within me
She buries a new memory I forget with time

She loves me
She loves me not
She loves me
She loved me lots
She loves me
Then she loves me not
She loves me
Then she loves me in spots
She loves me
Then her love for me tends to stop

You see, she got me feenin for a little smile
I've been hooked on her for a little while
I'm dependent on this girl
She's got me like a little child
I believe she loves me

But I believe her love for me tends to stop
She got me feeling a mess
Jealousy level types of stress
Logic of thoughts
Seems now to bleed out my chest
I'm corrupted
Tainted by her that much is obvious
It's all for lust
All for us
She got me building up my expectation
Along the banks of my raging denial
And she hurts me when she smiles
Twisted, twist it
For mix signals, she's got to be gifted

She loves me
She loves me not
She loves me
She loved me lots
She loves me
Then she loves me not
She loves me
Then she loves me in spots
She loves me
Then her love for me tends to stop

My life plans
She got me reevaluating
My fortress
She got me opening gates
And giving copies of the key
She's a mob star, definition of a G
I want her to be the woman for me
Got me spreading my branches like a tree
I want to be free
But she tears me down
Just as fast as she builds me up
Water overflows out of my once pristine cup
Trying to catch that heart, be heavy in her favor
But then

She loves me

Museum of My Soul

She loves me not
She loves me
She loved me lots
She loves me
Then she loves me not
She loves me
Then she loves me in spots
She loves me
Then her love for me tends to stop
She loves me
For me, I think she's got the hots
She loves me
So why does that love ever have to stop?

Cigarette

Baby, you're like a cigarette
It's something about the way
Your name lingers on my breath
It's something that you do
That makes me feel you
In the organs in my chest
It's like I'm addicted, and you're the nicotine
No cure for me, no Nicorette,
You've got me completely wrecked

Smoke all around
With you slowly but surely
My health was going down
It was fatal from the day we first met
This wasn't meant to be serious
Nothing long term
So I don't know why, somehow you, I let
You just kept coming around
I was foolish I'd always be down

Like a cigarette
Lighters lit you and you just kept burning
In the ashtray of my life, you kept turning
Filled with traces of smoke and dust
But it's really a reflection of us

It was like slowly but surely
You were causing me a disease
There was no room to break free
You didn't even give me the room to breathe
Oxygen was on short supply
It seemed that with or without you I'd die

Your love was like a cancer
With no cure, you provided me no answers
Just danger, dancing in my cells
Health failing, even a blind man could tell
I was in an emotional hell
I wasn't searching for love
But found one with no cure calling me
And you were the one that answered
Danger was on the other end, you didn't lie

You said "I'm no good for you friend"
But I didn't listen
All I did was pretend
This was supposed to be casual
I didn't think I would get addicted
I didn't think I wouldn't be able to fix it
I didn't think
That's it, I didn't
Because the signs were there
Nothing from me was hidden
To think, I didn't
Now

You're like a cigarette
With the taste of your flesh
Lingering on my breath
It's something about you
That's got me completely wrecked
I'm an addict of you
Supply me with some Nicorette
Light you up
I inhale the smoke that comes from you
I'm now out of breath
Nothing left, but an ashtray with a lit cigarette

Flames

Seems I love playing with fire
And I always end up burnt
And no matter the size of the blister
I go back for another turn
Dealing with so many scars
You'd think there be a lesson learned

Seems I love throwing my water on flames
Stream
A moist cloud of heat
Sweating and out of tune heartbeats, when we meet
I can't help it
You knocked me off my feet

Seems like, I like burning from desires
The heat of passion, momentary satisfaction
Engaging in bodily actions, naturally sensually
Makes sense to me
Seems I like things that aren't right for me
Dreams
In them is where my mind will be
Hoping I can tame wild flames
To float upon my oceans of emotions

But I love the danger of your flames
Wanting, burning up in your desires
I'm a willing participant in your blaze
Now I'm lost in your maze
Yet still, I'm willing to play the game

Cared

Told you I cared
But I didn't
Behind falling tears
Emotions are hard to remain hidden
Contemplating about life
Wondering about everything you didn't do
How did you come to this point?
This, this isn't you
This is something you shouldn't do
But yet here still you do

Told me you loved me
When you didn't
We both knew that to be a lie
Trying to keep this together
There are very little reasons why
Pretending to care
Afraid to leave cause of fear
Tears filled our eyes as at each other we stared
After being broken for so long
It's hard for us to be repaired
I cared
You cared
We had moments
When things together we shared

We said things
Things that we really didn't mean
Words cut, we were so mean
Heartache happens internally
And remain unseen
We said we cared
But care was absent in our beings
In the same physical space
But our minds in a different state

If we cared more
If we loved one another
Not just put up with each other
Then maybe here at the end of this cliff
We wouldn't be standing
Trying to come up with reasons not to jump

Taking all our trash to the front
Nowhere to dump
Plying up on the heart causing a lump
How did we get to this point?
Uncertainty, our only certainty
We felt we cared
But even that may have been a lie

Love's Game

I told you tales, I don't ever tell
I ain't been living good,
Want to be living well
So many mysteries, in a, lived in hell
I did the right things
The truth, well...
You're prettier than you were before
I closed my eyes and you opened yours
A broken heart doesn't open doors
I've been in love with...
Holding on to the thought
That it's physical
Spiritual, biblical
Lyrical

Hoping words with the heart somehow connects
I call 1-800 hoping your love I can collect
But we're in different worlds
These things no longer have an effect
Selected by pain
Heavy thunder, my heart pours into rain
Seems I was late, I missed love's train
Now I'm going insane
Officially a two-time loser at love's game

Can't Satisfy You

If I gave you the world
Would you take it?
If I gave you my heart
Would you break it?
Or would you accept it?
If I gave you my love
Would we make it?
Or just be two bodies together naked
If I couldn't give you all you desired
Would you still have for me that burning fire?

Can I satisfy you?
Confine to you
Love me, do you
Do you
Care
To that place let's take it there
This lustful existence you and I share
I rip open the cavity of my chest, so to you my
heart I could bare
My cries of an affectionate love
Do you even hear?
Are you too caught in your own world
To acknowledge I exist?
Blocking out everyone else's needs
To only cater to yours you insist
To the truth about you, I resist
Telling myself "no this cannot be"
After hearing
What those in my world were telling me
Tempted to catch a felony
To relax, I'll listen to these Coltrane melodies

I'd try to bring you the sun
You'd still turn from me and run
I'd try to move heaven and hell
And even if you loved or cared about me
You still wouldn't tell
This wasn't some teenage fascination
I've been with you through every situation
We've grown together, and yet I'm still all alone

I offered you the world
Why from me you didn't take it
I gave you my heart all you did was break it
I gave you my love, never once did we make it
Just bodies touching naked
I could have given you all that you desired
But for me in you doesn't burn that kind of fire

I can't satisfy you

Dysfunctional

I tried to paint you as a perfect picture
Knowing you were flawed
I fell in love with you
Knowing I shouldn't have gotten involved
You started the pursuit
How quickly that revolved
Went from asking questions
About the direction of our commitment
To you now questioning our commitment
You see the excitement at the beginning
Had me all hazy
You seemed perfect, candy and daisies

My past told me to run
Or at least put a lock on my feelings.
For that is what I always did
A screen protector on my heart
Catch all the cracks
Where I could just peel it off
When we were through
I would be as good as new
But then I found you
I don't what kind of magic you had
But you cast a spell
And sure enough, I fell
I've fallen into the darkest corner
Of this relationship cell
Reluctant to break free
You've made believe I want this misery
Gaslighted, more it seems that way as I write it

You make me feel like you love me
I'm trying to hold on
While you're running away
It was subtle before
But the disrespect keeps coming my way
Under the guise of some emotional distress
Caused by an EX
But you're really an asshole
Let's put this mess to rest

I'm emotionally spent, so I've decided to give up
Cause I don't know
If a relationship should be this hard
Can't get rid of the feeling
That you're either unsure or ashamed of me
Was it the fear of being alone
Or love that's gotten us this far
Cause after this much time
I shouldn't be questioning these things
After so much time I shouldn't be questioning
And afraid to let you know how I feel
If you're still in love with your past
Let's keep it real
Let's set both our lives free
Let's work on the dysfunctional parts
Starting with our dysfunctional hearts
But there might be no cure
For the dysfunction that is our souls
With this type of corruption
I don't know if either of us
Can ever again be pure

Savage Heart

You hold me, hostage
Cut my heart into pieces like that of savage
These scars can't be hidden by simple bandages
But somehow I manage
Holds my heart hostage
And puts it up for ransom
Belittles me, quite a grand sum
I can't romance you
Call your phone, never get an answer

However, I can't leave
Shackles my heart
Using every trick up your sleeves
Your charm does my mind
But the body no harm
You tell me things, why do I believe?
You tell me you love me and I'm relieved
I've become so easy to deceive

You have me going through the motions
Playing with my emotions
Floating on your lies
You've got my heart, and I've got my pride
I live with a notion
Of you making me feel less than I am
Thought I knew who was
But that decision is no longer in my hands
I feel small and that's where our situation stands

I can't do this any no longer
I've got to be stronger
Every time I tell myself it's over
You're right over my shoulders
You just seem to get bolder
Whispering in my ears telling me
"baby we're not over"
I start to think that the pain I feel is not real
For a brief moment
I start to believe that you care
So I roll over
And we just start this drama all over

Kidnapped my heart
I was a runaway from the start
Somehow you captured this runaways'
Broken parts
Stockholm Syndrome
Palindrome
Back and forth you still don't change
Why do I keep taking this crap?
I'm like a dog feeding off your scraps
I'm in love with you like that

I keep asking what kind of life will I lead
If I leave?
I want to believe that you're the one
Even when you lie and cheat
My pride won't accept defeat
My skin you're very much underneath
Burns my soul, you are the heat

You hold my heart hostage
Beats it up like a punching bag
Emotions battered and bruised
My mind confused
No wonder I keep getting used
I want to win but always lose
Love isn't a choice, you can't often choose
I never doubt you
Just myself

Will I ever tame your savage heart?
Got to let you go, I've got to leave
Failing to start
Can't see us apart
Losing this fight, these matters of the heart
You rip my heart into pieces
Like that of a savage
And these wounds will never heal
But somehow I manage
I'm in love with a savage
Who's slowly tearing me apart

No Good For Me

You're no good for me
But from you, I don't want to run
Making decisions with the heart
So the mind already knows the outcome

You're no good for me
But the feelings you give to me
Those feelings, feel so good to me
But, you're no good for me
But I can't picture anybody else
But you loving me
You're no good
I should leave you, really I should
But really I don't know if I could
I always said if the opportunity presented itself
I would take it
But it has several times
But right back into your arms I start running
Foolish me
The heart never learns
It keeps taking a beating
But keeps coming back for seconds, thirds
My head always tells me to stop
You're no good for me
But your lovemaking has been so good to me
It does good for me
While emotionally there's nothing about you
That's good for me

You're no good
Make you better, wish I could
You're not the one
But I want you to be
The heartache
The stress
The headaches, depressed
These are a few of the things
Our union gives to me

I'm drained mentally
Full of battle scars
Up late

Spending time alone drinking in an empty bar
Frequent visits with different brands of alcohol
Dial tone
It's you I call
Voicemail
I leave a message
Saying all types of things

You're no good for me
But from you, I don't want to be
Don't take your love from me
Even if the love you give isn't just for me
You're bad you see
But from your love, I don't want to be freed

You're no good
I shouldn't love you
I should move on
Keep strong
But your loving is so good
The hold is so strong
My thoughts of leaving you
To I can never hold on
Phantoms of the past
Half-empty is my glass
I don't know how
We make this broken thing last

I'm still waiting for the right one
The right one to fill my half-empty metaphor
But how can I?
When all you do is take from me
I'm now a desert of emotions
Lacking passion, and desire
I'm now a frequent flyer
Carrying a lot of emotional baggage
You've got me damaged

You're no good for me
But I can't leave
At times I feel like I can't breathe

But your touch is so good
Trapped by you sexually
Mentally it's not you
I know there's something wrong with me
So there's no end near for you and me
Constantly asking myself the question, Why?

It's the sex
All because of what I think is love
But really it's the fact, I know how broken being
away from you I'd be
My mind says to run
But my heart won't let that be
So I'm fighting the reasons of logic, to be
With a person that's no good for me

Danger to myself

I'm a danger to myself
But I don't need nobody's help
Cause I don't need nobody else, but you
I don't think you understand
What you've got my mind going through
I can't sleep at nights as soon
As I close my eyes all I think about is you
Look what you've got my heart going through
I'm lost, can somebody tell me what I'm gon' do
When all I can do is think about me running away from you
I'm hiding out in the open
Hoping that you don't see me
Coping with these feelings that you leave me
But why would you leave me?
I'm gonna be fine I don't need you, to need me
Believe me
If you leave
You're gonna want me back when you see me

I don't need nobody's help
I'd find me somebody else
It was never a good ideal
Loving someone more than I did myself
But will heartbreak help?
It might teach me how the broken heal...
Danger to myself, I've got that broken feel
But I'm okay
I've still got my health, the greatest kind of wealth

But I'm going to be okay
Even though I might be a stranger amongst friends
Even though I try to act strong, it's really just pretend
I'm in need of someone's help
I can't live this way I've become a danger to myself
I need somebody's help
I'm in need of somebody else
It's not just me
So does everybody else

The Heart Of A Broken Fool

She never loved me
Just the idea of all the things I can do for her
She looked me in the eyes
And told me I was never true to her
Now doing this shit was nothing too new to her
Because she's been breaking hearts
Since she was a kid
A fight with her you could never win
She knew how to get under anybody's skin
With her, not a man could get in
Her body count was larger
Than the planet Jupiter
But that didn't stop many men
From trying to Cupid her
Looked at them and wonder
Could they get any stupider
Na, she just got sweeter
She was fine
Ticketing any man that would park to meet her

She cried with few tears
Whispered within my fooled ears
A devil within them glued stares
She's quite something hard to compare

She said I was never there
Said I lied and never cared
That's when it became clear
That she saw me as nothing
More than trash surrounded by flies
I was buried within her lies
She could have easily disposed of me
Never wanted to get close to me
She never loved me
Just all the things I could do for her
I was from Mars
But her list of broken hearts
Was greater than the planet Jupiter
She does this daily this ain't nothing new to her
I was next on her list
Couldn't believe I was going out like this
She had targets to hit, which she did not miss

I wondered if there was room for me
On her world of broken hearts
After all, I wasn't the first
But the latest to be torn apart
I guess I'm about to find out
What loving like a fool is all about
While discovering why breaking hearts
Is truly her art
And why every man that ever loved her
Played a part in breaking his own heart
But this is just a tale of the heart of a broken
fool, playing a game with broken rules
And as a man, I was always going to lose
So there's no sympathy for this broken fool

Thin Line Between Love and Hate

Like the song says there's a thin line
Between love and hate
She's willing to throw the fine china at my face
I watch them break
I don't know how much more of this shit I can take
Fine line yeah that's putting it lightly
It's a tight rope me and her are walking nightly
Sparkles fly she's willing to fight me
She's got an attitude, of someone she reminds me
Oh yeah that's right, me
We both got tempers, jealous by nature
Just as fast as we say I love you
We'll scream out I hate you

It's a thin line between love and hate
I know some of you can relate
Relationships are a trip
Movies advertise this as being great
But I'm only getting half the satisfaction
I want a refund
This ain't fun
One of us will be in the hospital
Before it's all said and done
Yeah Intensive care, a right to fear

She throwing things at me
Dishes, cup, picture frames
Calling the lord, and cussing my name
She even smashed the TV screen
See this type of jealousy is unseen
So green the hulk would blush
She throws rocks to my car windows
Emotional that's the way she's always been though
Acts first, then listens to reasons later
I love this woman
But lawd knows how much I really hate her
See we fight and have makeup sex after
Our relationship isn't a fairy tale
No happily ever after
Our story ends with a preacher
Or pastor and a funeral parlor
Strong feelings for each other we do harbor

There's a thin line between love and hate
And I love to hate
Every man she talks to that I don't know
I give her hell
A fight breaks out
A knife out of kitchen draw, she takes out
For a rational love, our hearts both bleeds out
But we're insane
I think that's something we both found out

A thin line
In the heart, love was in mine
On the mind, hate is what you would find
We went from loving and caring
To now hiding and no longer sharing
Now we're in the same room talking
But neither of our ears is hearing
To each other, we're never listening
Went from saying I love you
To not acknowledging we know one another
Went from being together
To now in the company of others
Went from peace
To now having a war with each other
Went from trying to kill one another
To having each other's back
It's just as crazy and confusing as that
A love where our hearts are both black
Fill with misunderstandings and confusing the facts
It makes no sense but our relationship is like that

It's a thin line between love and hate
It's a game of give and take
Until someone completely breaks
It's a thin line, it's always there
Even if that relationship feels great
That line can always be crossed
And joy and lives could be lost
There's a thin line between love and hate

Something about Our Relationship

Baby trying to playing me like TiVo
Trying rewind the situation, wait where did she go
We're trying to save our pride, our fragile little egos
Claim the pain you feel is too much
And you're trying to get over Dee though
Everything is going downhill, we on a steep slope
But our speed slow
It seems like this all started with me, so
We can't see eye to eye
We're both trying to get our piece of the pie
It's like about anything little thing, you and I would lie
We gave it a good try
We were warned, love could die
Now we're here, the goodbyes
We sure did have some good times
Our relationship, filled with love crimes
Sentenced multiple times
But I'm breaking out can't give you a lifetime
Being together is toxic
Acid rain melts my metal frame
I hate to breakup
This the last time
There won't be any kind of makeup
In love, my faith's up
Looking for a character, but I can't be your hero
I can't save you and save me too
I use to, but I no longer love you
It's just some things about our relationship
I can never get used to
So it's just best to lose us
It's best I lose you
Before I lose me, and any sense of who I am
So goodbye, baby

Cheater

She calls me a cheat
She calls me a liar
But I can't admit that
I guess my pants on fire
Being faithful, I don't think
I have that thing that's required
So any accusations she brings to me
I'll deny her

She says I'm a cheat
She tells her friends I'm a liar
But she won't leave me
Her intentions are deflated like flat tires
See her cries, hurts
But telling her these lies works
I get it I'm no good
On the side doing my girl dirt
But these other girls flirt
And I'm weak, I've got no will power
They lead back to the bed
And there's no need for alcohol in my head
But a little is never bad

She calls me a cheat
That may be the truth
But I don't think I'm a liar
But they say you end up burnt
When you start playing with fire
And I'm the number one arson
Her pain, yeah I'm the supplier
I know she's a good girl
Couldn't imagine her with another
It'd hurt too much
I couldn't handle her doing these things
Just like me
But that's just like me,
To want things that only works for me

She says I'm a cheat
Sorry baby I'm a liar
I know I'll never meet another girl like her
But I like her, her, her and her

I can't help myself
I wouldn't feel like myself
Baby, please don't leave me by myself

I'm a cheat
Yes, baby, I'm a liar
I'll admit it now
My pants were on fire
Only chasing my desires
Being faithful, that's the hard part
Half-hearted, don't want us to be parted
Our life, don't want to lose what we started
So I'm wishing for the will to not cheat
Even when these girls throw themselves
At my feet
But if I can't please don't let me get caught
Cause from her love this cheater
Doesn't want to get lost

Museum of My Soul
The Time It Took:

Ending

First To Say Goodbye

I hate to let you go, but I've gotta let you go
Those are the thoughts running through my mind
Can't bring myself to tell you those lines
We've been together for some time
But it seems us together is no longer fine
We both know that this love has expired
We've run out of time
We know we should say goodbye

But neither one of us wants to be the first to say goodbye

We've had some good years
Love at times can be so unkind
And I'll always remember the good times
We know, we know this has to end
When we started and became way more than friends
We've come a long away
We've reached the end, the end of the line
Yes the end, the end of our time

But neither one of us wants to be the first to say goodbye

I don't want to be the one
The first one to say our goodbyes
You know that love hurts, it's that way sometimes
I'll always love you, but you know love runs its course in due time
You'll stay with me forever, in my heart, soul, and mind
I don't want to be the first, no, no, no
But we both know it's time

But neither one of us wants to be the first to say goodbye
I said neither one of us, wants to be the first to say goodbye

Tale of The Broken Hearted

I see how it is
I know you don't want me anymore
But you really hurt me
When you walked out that door
It was early in the morning somewhat pass four
You knew I loved you
So much my heart did adore
I gave you anything you wanted
As long as I could afford
You were worth so much more
It wasn't for the money
I just loved you, honey
And I know they say loves for fools
Well I guess I was your dummy
Because I knew you loved me
And that's worth more than any money
I wanted to be somebody
Oh I need your body
Because you were more than just somebody

I knew why you left me
But here's where my life be
And it hurts because my life left me
And it hurts when your soul is taken
That's what theft be
I felt like dying
You standing at the door bags packed crying
Said you could take no more
The part about me lying, I said "I wasn't lying"
But this was time I was just buying
Trying to keep away the feeling
Of my heart dying
I can't take losing you
What's a man to do?
I'm just a man
These things should be nothing new
You can't just leave me here feeling blue
Standing her missing you
Seeing you in another man's arms
Wouldn't be easy
And the world just seems to get colder for me
So breezy

And when they say "things will get better"
It sounds so cheesy
Because mine will never get back
To what it used to be, easy

Time to change lanes
Time to change plains
Can't continue to live my life in the fast lane
The past doesn't change
But causes such frustration
I'm left all alone
I'm left with nothing in this world
I'm nothing but a lonely stone
Made to stay here forever where I laid my sins
I tried rolling away
But that change won't come for me today

You left me broken-hearted
My only feeling since we've parted
Wishing I could restart this
But in life losers miss hitting that target
Where the heart is
So I guess no more me and you
Just you, me, and whoever your heart's with
See history possesses such mysteries
But not with me
With me, it means what we are history
And with it a life filled with his stories
Fill with so much faults glory
So many faults stories
Now there are no more stories
There's no glory without you
Because you were my favorite part
Of many stories

Felony of the Mind

It was a felony of the mind
You were always at the bottom of the line
But you were always the bottom line
And at the bottom I'm
Still trying to tell myself you're worth it
I get it, I know what we have here isn't perfect
But it'd hurt if
We didn't even try

It was a felony of the mind
In my head, I'm doing the maximum time
It was a stupid crime
I kissed the lips of someone that wasn't you
Brush the hair from her face, I wasn't true
And you caught me in the act
Of something I said I wouldn't do
I'm guilty
Brought a stranger into our home
I'm so filthy

The pain of that day still fills me, with agony
It sounds strange now
But I miss the way you used to nag at me
I miss the simple things you'd do
I'm upset at myself
Cause quite simply I hate missing you

It was a felony of the mind
Playing that moment over and over in my mind
It's locked in there playing all the time
I wasn't perfect, with anything I did
And I decided to cross the line
I guess I was too comfortable
Maybe I didn't understand
What it meant to be happy
It never even crossed my mind
I was doing wrong
Until you walked in that door
And saw what was going on
I'm the cause for our destruction
No chance of reconstruction
Weak fell for another female's seduction

I'm looking for excuses
Some lie I can tell myself to explain
Why I'd cheat on my lady
The only women I've ever loved
But I was selfish
Now I'm living the life of a shellfish

It was a felony of the mind
A lapse in my moral judgment
I knew when the gavel went down
What the judge meant
Just wish it hadn't had to end that way
I wish I didn't throw our life and love away
No longer will this mind of mine be free
A felon locked away in Thought's Penitentiary
Solitary confinement, heavy heart realignment
Because without you
My life is completely empty

I Can't Take It

I can't take it
Every thought I have you make it
Every emotion you break it
My heart you staked it
Every day I wake it's just a cycle of pain
Of not having you here
Not having you near
Not having you care

I can't take it
The tears I cry makes it so real
These feelings I feel
These wounds won't heal
I just loved you, it was no big deal
My emotions I find it so hard to conceal
But you made me feel, to you things I could reveal
Never knew my heart you would peel
You stole it, then destroyed it
Joy it's something I don't feel any more
It's because of you I've lost it

I can't take this
My heart
You're the one that always breaks it
When the time comes
Makes it so difficult to put it back together
And even though I'm mad at you
When I look at you
It's like I start falling right back in love with you
I don't know what I am supposed to do
I can't even bring my eyes to look at you

I can't take this
That's why I'm shedding these tears
Wishing I could replace these memories of you that I see so clear
I wish I could forget the way I feel about you
And how it hurts not having you here
I can't take this
That why I'm going need help
Wiping away each and every one of these falling tears

Museum of My Soul

The week was long, finally, it's the weekend
It's been three months now and we still ain't speaking
Remember when we were together
Holding each other while we were sleeping

Back when my papers were ink free
And my mind was thinking clearly
Now I'm here writing my thoughts with free pens
The ink all around you've got me drowning in the deep end

My mind isn't straight no more
I'm having trouble sleeping
Wondering about the secrets you were keeping
Since you left me, I've been weak, weeping

Being alone is trouble and without you
My loneliness has doubled
My world just in rubbles
People say life is tough, bull
Cause my life was easy with you in it
And now that you're gone,
The same isn't what it used to be
It's become different

No longer friends we just started a trend that led to the end... of us
No senses it's left me speechless grief-stricken
Wondering if in my lifetime I'd find love
But did love find us forbidden

But that's the story of life
Memories, rewritten to remember the good times
While trying to lose the sad ones
But I know that the wounds will just deepen
At nighttime wondering, if my world will be different when I wake up
It's a dream I'm just sleeping, I keep telling myself

I want to ease the way it felt
I miss the person who changed my world
But they're gone for good messed up my chance at happiness
Crappy, this feeling might hurt a little bit
And I don't see the benefits of you leaving me
I'm broken nowhere to run, I've got nothing to
I just can't stand this feeling of being alone without you

Black and Blue

My heart is now black and blue
From fighting these feelings I have for you
It hurts so bad I don't know what to do
This is a fight I seem to always lose
Forfeit because I never learn the rules
I had my heart broken before
But this hurts so much more
It shook me to my core
Because after my heart was broken once before
I thought I could love no more
Could never trust someone like I did before
But I saw something in you, others didn't have on you
I thought you would make my life anew
Never knew you would have my heart black and blue

This should be nothing new
I always somewhat knew that you would leave me here somewhat blue
But I try to hide it deep inside
And I always knew you were never true
I just took a mental picture
I just looked at your crew
Now I'm wishing I didn't lie to myself
Because you got my heart so black and blue

Love is a war I keep losing
And ever battle I was in wasn't of my choosing
They say you can't choose who you love
So when your heart is ripped out and torn in two
It hurts like hell it's supposed to
I suppose you, you knew I loved you
Because of that, I had blind trust in you

You play the game too well and my heart is hurting
Breaking can you tell
But I'm going to be okay I'm going to be well
Because after living in these hells
I don't know if I can love again
But I did learn loves a game, and I'm a two-time loser
But this time I' ma win
That's all I can try to do, this time anew
Because I can't always live my life as the one whose heart is always black and blue
Next time I'll win
Next time I'll know just what to do

Realizing

Realizing I'm the one that's broken
Struggling to reopen
Can't heal
Getting another one of you, my way of coping
I was hoping
That all my troubles were external
And the world was to blame
Can't trust you, because of a guilty mind
Framed pictures of the things I've done
I now project them upon you
The anxiety of falling in love
With fears, my trust issues
Realize and see
I'm the one that's not completely together
Waking every morning hoping my emotional skies
Aren't filled with bad weather
Never knowing whether these fears are real
Broken me, struggling to stay in the moment see...
And not worrying about the past
Not getting anxious of a future that may never be
This is a hard lesson for me
I've got to enjoy the moments
For they move too fast.
All things go and come
And just like the goods ones
The bad ones too will also pass

I Used to Love Her

I used to love her
But about me, she wasn't feeling the same
I swear catching emotions about someone who didn't
Is almost insane
These feelings are driving me to pain
A broken heart wears you down like heavy chains
Standing in the heavy rain
Thought you found the one and heaven came
But that wasn't the case
And the change I wanted wasn't the phase
Showing the right places for a fee
They said love's blind, but I just wanted to see
Why the girl I was building with
Feelings weren't building for me
My so call love was towering over her ground level of indifference
I thought in my life you'd be the difference
I thought we were over that, we already did friends
Looking to free ends
Failing at the game of love for me has become too frequent
Again insane you see
Crazy about the feeling you gave to me
Freedom of heart
Being broken apart
But this journey of someday finding my soul
Mate, I had to start

The Sin of Love

Lust, passion, possession, and jealousy
Wrapped in the package of love
Is what the world keeps selling me
Infatuated with the fear of letting go
Fear of never knowing if we can find this feeling again
The feeling we've gained
Will we feel it the same
Holding on to a memory
But no longer can we go on as we
We planted seeds
We were weeds hoping to turn into trees
Our growth couldn't be,
Is what society told you about us
And I was in a rut, rusted and stuck
Patience ran thin,
Your good graces I was no longer in
Falling in love our original sin
So I guess this is the end of *U N I* and finally I see...*T. Y.*

Hurt

I try to take the hurt with the pain
The sun with the rain
Not having you is almost insane
Not having you here
My world's an out of control moving train
Beat up my heart, placed my emotions in chains
Nothing will ever be the same
What do you do when you found your perfect one?
What do you do when that joy walks away?

I've been thinking heavily about you since we last spoke
You hurt me, no joke
And this feeling runs deep into the trenches of my soul
Every time I think I'm over you
Memories come rushing back ten folds
They hit me where it hurts must, shadows of you
You've now gone ghost
Seems like just yesterday you were in my arms, close
I don't want to accept that drink was our last toast
I don't get
We were cool, what did I do wrong
What kind of vibe you be flowing on
On the outside this hurt, won't be showing long
But inside my chest, a heavy heart has got me a mess
I guess life has given me my first test
Stress, stress, I'm stressing
Hard to understand what good things
I'll learn from this lesson
Except how to be broken, mentally into pieces
Constantly thinking what your life is now missing
You've got me rattled, my emotions
You've changed, and with my pride, I'm in a battle
I'm defeated, upset kind of heated
You've made up your mind
Your heart I can never win
Another replay of a situation I was already in

Untimely

She said she couldn't love me the way I deserved to
I was broken-hearted, no one to turn to
I was one that turned two, then back to one again
You know how when you're feeling pain?
Hoping that feelings change
Tided, up in my emotions
Fell into that ocean
Floating on desires that I couldn't catch
Long days at sea I couldn't rest
Thinking why you do this to me
I want you
But you want me to be free
Time is heartbreak's referee
But what a worse time this could be
My mind is racing, my head in a basin
Your love I'm no longer tasting
And every thought I have of you
My heart once again starts breaking

Love Depraved

What happened to your heart?
Why did we start so good, and became so staunch?
Why are deception and desire still the forces tearing us apart
What started so bright has now turned so dark
What brought us together drove us apart

What happened to your heart?
They say emotions manifest from the mind, not the heart
Overthinking caused the relationship to sink
In the bottles, we started drinking
And we link things to our childhood
And how we were raised
Because how can we give love, when we were deprived
It's hard to give something that you never had in your life
But your expectations are manufactured
Things from an AD
You don't know the real thing
Our love was depraved
You just want what you never had
Hoping maybe one day you'll find it

What happened to your heart?
Were we wrong?
The way that we started
Unable to finish, because the self has been left undone
So there's no surprise with this terrible outcome

So what happened to my heart
It's been shattered, broken in pieces
Slowly trying to figure out where these puzzle pieces go
So until I'm whole, I've got to be careful not to break others
And that's how my story will be sold
Tears on pillows, that keep secrets
It won't tell a soul, that these tears belong to a man
Whose heart has a hole and has been blackened

After The Breakup

I've been running from what is going on, on my insides
Knowing my bad feelings to be true
But kept it on the inside
But it didn't go away, just got bigger in sizes
Manifests its self into my reality, oh sin, pride
The universe has been showing me truth
Can't tell lies with eyes
Rejection breeds new interest
But not from love, but an ego bruised from being let go
But you had already given up
But wouldn't give it up
Signs of physical stress
Can't eat, can't rest
You needed this, you can now breathe
New breath
You can once again be content
You did more, it's your time to do less
You'll learn from this
Grow from it to be a better you
When the time is right, the type of love you need will find you
But these are 4 AM thoughts mind you
You really got to work hard to just to find you
To go back to a *you* from a *we*
From that relationship cord break free
After the breakup
There were no cries of why me
Just thoughts that I'll be healing
And the residual scars the pain will be leaving

Mirror, Mirror

Our problem was, that I saw you as a mirror
A reflection of who I was
All my shortcomings you reflected onto me
In you, I saw reflected how I could do better
Our problem was
Your view of me was not the same
I was only a window
A visual passage to your next destination
The place you wanted to be
The love wasn't there for me
I was only the glass in the way
Any mistake or "red flag"
You saw it as your cue to
"Break in case of emergency"
Exiting right through this window
Running away to your next place of refuge
Because it's easier to run away
Than to actually face our problems
Work through
You say you love me, but do you?
What does that word even mean to you?
I was putting myself on a time line
To live up to something you won't give
Only excuses and confusion offered up
But I took it because I was in love
I figured out I'm broken too, always chasing
Seems I like the challenge of making one commit
When they say they couldn't
Maybe it's my ego saying
"I'm gonna make you love me"
All the while running from those affections
When directed towards me
I learned my faults in all the fray
I now know the difference
Between love and confusion
That's what you offered to me
In a pretty package
But if we're being honesty love this wasn't
Just a fear of being alone
I had no real chance of truly getting your love
I've accepted the facts, and I'm letting you go
I had to end this Act

Move onto the next scene
Find my true queen
Or as you would say the right one for me
Now I know what I attract
I've got to change my energy and thoughts
Only then will I find the one
That's aligned with me

Mirror, mirror
Tell me what I've been doing wrong
Because through teary eyes
I no longer have clear sight
Mirror, mirror
Is it fair at all
To want to pickup the phone
Give her a call
Or should I let go, and let grow
Mirror, mirror
Would you please help me
I can still hear her
I don't want to hear her
I see her reflection looking back at me
In you miserable mirror

Fonder

They say absence makes the heart grow fonder
And each moment without you, makes me wish
When I had you I held on a little longer
Wrapped my arms around you more tightly
Kiss you more like we, were still teenage lovers
Then right here with me, you just might be
This is what I think about nightly
Loving you rightly
My love for you just might be
Like me, getting stronger
I'm missing you, my emotions got me sinking
taking me under
Cause I'm not with you any longer

They say absence makes the heart grows fonder
They say if you love someone, then you got to
let them go
And if they come back that means they know
They know nobody else could love them more
And your love should grow
My heart beats, like old wooden floors, creaks
Meaning internally I'm weak

Absence makes the heart grows fonder
And since the last time, I said that
You've been away from me, a moment longer
My heart beats harder
The pain in my chest stronger
Cause I'm not with you
I had to let you go
I hope that lets you know
I love you so much
But I want it to be reciprocal
It's hurting right now, in the long run
I hope it's beneficial
So if you don't come back I'll live with the fact
It had to end like that

We don't always get what we want
And that's even more true, now that you're gone
I don't know if it's temporary or forever
But I've got to move on

I miss you, that's my issue
I thought we could get through, anything
I'm wishing you'd come back
But I'm done wishing
I'm done with that
I want you back, but I have to deal with the fact
You're gone, no longer in my arms
No longer will I be flattered by your charm
You and I are no longer
And absence makes me wonder what we had
That makes me mad
Because I don't know if I can have it back
So I'm letting go
I just want you to know I still love you so
I hope apart, we both grow

Thinking About You

I think of you sometimes
You know when I'm alone and just thinking
Memories of you just sneak in
Reminiscing about you
But I'm not drifting

I think of you sometimes
You know of what we had
It was good sometimes
It wasn't all bad

I think of you sometimes
When I'm in the park
And lovers pass me by
It takes me back to a time
When that was you and I
Enjoyed nature as much
As I enjoyed seeing your smile

I think of you
When the world around me becomes quiet
Then in my head memories of you cause a riot
Thoughts start rushing in
Memories of your kisses and your touches
They begin
I miss you much is, the way I feel
I think of you, but why should you care
It's no big deal
We're no longer together
Why should you care how I feel

I think of you sometimes
Whenever I'm alone
And have a moment to think
You always seem to sneak in
And for those moments
I can't get you out my mind
Out of my system
I think of you sometimes
And the love we had
Sometimes have become often

The Love We Had

I guess I get it
I wasn't worthy
Whether it was in looks or trust
Hold up now I'm getting too wordy
I'm confused for many reasons
But the biggest one is why I'm not with you
A year has passed
And I'm still thinking about you
Why we fell apart?
I haven't got a clue
But I'm busy thinking, thinking about you
What it is that you do now?
Since my eyes have left you
I'm still thinking about the past
And the things we did last

I saw a picture of you just the other day
Seem like you moved on
Got someone new to fill my place
Seems every thought about me got erased
I know my place
You're not even thinking about me
Well at least not out loudly
Never once did you ask a damn thing about me
I guess that's the pattern with everyone
Who moved on without me
The girls I was once with find love after me
I'm merely a place holder
A divider in a disorganized folder
Can't believe how true my words were
When this I told her

I guess I get it now
I'll let it go
I guess my mystery of feelings
I'll never show
But when I see you in photos with someone else
It hurts me though
Cause what it feels to be completely yours
I'll never know
But that thought I'll let it go
I've got to, that's the only way to grow

Only way I can go
Now

Never thought I'd fall in love
Never knew I could feel its pain
I guess what they say about heartache is true
I saw the girl I was with, a year later and still
I felt the same
I felt a pain in my chest
I think its love no less
I'm such a mess
I feel ashamed
She was with another man
And my heart still feels the strain
I never knew such pain
Saw a photograph of her with another man
And she looked happy
And from that moment I knew
I'd never be the same
I'd just have to find a way
To make her mine again
I can only hope something inside her about me
Feels the same
All I can do is hope
That false comfort could help me coup
I miss her
But that's something to myself I must keep
She moved on, I've got to do the same
Or the thoughts of her with another man
Will drive me insane
It's different, but when you lose love
It's true
Your world isn't supposed to feel the same

HMM

Hmm
When you lose a good thang
And realize it ain't ever coming back

Hmm
Would you look at that
You weren't looking forward for us
Now you looking back
Would you look at that

Hmm
You lost a good thing
Self-inflicted suffering
Emotions, you played yourself
On harp strings
No harbouring bad feelings
Life is about its peaks, valleys and hurt feeling
But you'll feel that pain now
Take with you all your half-ass reasons
It's cold now
But you'll have a yearlong winter season

Hmm
When you lose the best
It goes without saying for the rest of your life
You'll be settling for less

Hmm

A Break

I took a break
Needed some time to connect back with the divine
You know get a lot of things off Dee's mind
Had my heart broken about three times
By the same muse
New shit played over old news
I needed time to meditate
Get some new views on life
A broken heart can make you do that sometimes

I needed space, cleared out the old
And made a new reality
Love can make you do some crazy things
Compromise your integrity
Because of a fear of losing it
Just to end up losing it
Realizing our fears become our reality
I needed a break from myself
To become once again myself

I felt the heaviness of my soul weighing me down
The girl I gave my heart to was returning it to me
She could no longer love me now
I cried internally for weeks
My heart shedding each tear
I knew this was the most likely outcome
But I like challenges
So I tried to make a different one
But I learned an important lesson
Be with who wants to be with you
You don't want to hear certain phrases
When the relationship ends, like
I just don't think you were meant for me
It hits a little different
When you're invested in the person
From whose lips those words exit
An insecurity of value takes effect
A bruised hubris

I took a break
Came to terms with all my mistakes

I learned my lessons
Realizing the older I get the less I know
Yet still
I'll move forward like a child with a big heart
And a curious mind
That's the only way I know, how
So like a tree water me with your compassion
And enjoy my gifts
These fruits of love

Final Goodbye

This is my final goodbye
I gave us a really good try
I lied to me
I was not blind, Ice cold seas
These waters were not for me
I don't know how many more ways
I could take you telling me
You do not want me

Passion filled doubts, is on what I overdose
Playing emotional defense
Taking shots to my pride
Tapping into levels of insecurities I didn't know I have
Made me feel less than worthy
But this doing was all me
I wasn't prepared
It's just the picture in my mind and reality doesn't always align
I don't know why I endured this
The universe kept putting challenges in front of us
It's way of telling me to leave

In my head, I made up a fantasy I still want to believe
That we had something special, achieved
What have I done?
Fell into something, that I questioned each day
Was this ever really love?
Stuck in my head are ideas
But was love something we actually felt?
Or was this just an unhealthy attachment?
With the ideas of what being in love meant
I guess I'll never really know
But I can't stay occupying spaces where I'm not welcomed
I've got to go and navigate new seas
For I've been here before
Only to once again brush up against love's shores
Back in a relationship once more

Museum of My Soul
is now

Come back again to visit

Dnice Keoma

CPSIA information can be obtained
at www.ICGtesting.com
Printed in the USA
BVHW010900190320
575432BV00004B/42